My College Visit Journal

THIS JOURNAL BELONGS TO:

DATE

COLLEGE

INITIAL IMPRESSION

POSITIVES

NEGATIVES

PROGRAMS OF STUDY

DORMS

LIBRARY

CAMPUS DINING

STUDENT LIFE

ADDITIONAL NOTES

APPLY?

APPLICATION DEADLINE

SCHOLARSHIP & FINANCIAL AID INFO

DATE

COLLEGE

INITIAL IMPRESSION

POSITIVES

NEGATIVES

PROGRAMS OF STUDY

DORMS

LIBRARY

CAMPUS DINING

STUDENT LIFE

ADDITIONAL NOTES

APPLY?

APPLICATION DEADLINE

SCHOLARSHIP & FINANCIAL AID INFO

DATE

COLLEGE

INITIAL IMPRESSION

POSITIVES

NEGATIVES

PROGRAMS OF STUDY

DORMS

LIBRARY

CAMPUS DINING

STUDENT LIFE

ADDITIONAL NOTES

APPLY?

APPLICATION DEADLINE

SCHOLARSHIP & FINANCIAL AID INFO

DATE

COLLEGE

INITIAL IMPRESSION

POSITIVES

NEGATIVES

PROGRAMS OF STUDY

DORMS

LIBRARY

CAMPUS DINING

STUDENT LIFE

ADDITIONAL NOTES

APPLY?

APPLICATION DEADLINE

SCHOLARSHIP & FINANCIAL AID INFO

DATE

COLLEGE

INITIAL IMPRESSION

POSITIVES

NEGATIVES

PROGRAMS OF STUDY

DORMS

LIBRARY

CAMPUS DINING

STUDENT LIFE

ADDITIONAL NOTES

APPLY?

APPLICATION DEADLINE

SCHOLARSHIP & FINANCIAL AID INFO

DATE

COLLEGE

INITIAL IMPRESSION

POSITIVES

NEGATIVES

PROGRAMS OF STUDY

DORMS

LIBRARY

CAMPUS DINING

STUDENT LIFE

ADDITIONAL NOTES

APPLY?

APPLICATION DEADLINE

SCHOLARSHIP & FINANCIAL AID INFO

DATE

COLLEGE

INITIAL IMPRESSION

POSITIVES

NEGATIVES

PROGRAMS OF STUDY

DORMS

LIBRARY

CAMPUS DINING

STUDENT LIFE

ADDITIONAL NOTES

APPLY?

APPLICATION DEADLINE

SCHOLARSHIP & FINANCIAL AID INFO

DATE

COLLEGE

INITIAL IMPRESSION

POSITIVES

NEGATIVES

PROGRAMS OF STUDY

DORMS

LIBRARY

CAMPUS DINING

STUDENT LIFE

ADDITIONAL NOTES

APPLY?

APPLICATION DEADLINE

SCHOLARSHIP & FINANCIAL AID INFO

DATE

COLLEGE

INITIAL IMPRESSION

POSITIVES

NEGATIVES

PROGRAMS OF STUDY

DORMS

LIBRARY

CAMPUS DINING

STUDENT LIFE

ADDITIONAL NOTES

APPLY?

APPLICATION DEADLINE

SCHOLARSHIP & FINANCIAL AID INFO

DATE

COLLEGE

INITIAL IMPRESSION

POSITIVES

NEGATIVES

PROGRAMS OF STUDY

DORMS

LIBRARY

CAMPUS DINING

STUDENT LIFE

ADDITIONAL NOTES

APPLY?

APPLICATION DEADLINE

SCHOLARSHIP & FINANCIAL AID INFO

DATE

COLLEGE

INITIAL IMPRESSION

POSITIVES

NEGATIVES

PROGRAMS OF STUDY

DORMS

LIBRARY

CAMPUS DINING

STUDENT LIFE

ADDITIONAL NOTES

APPLY?

APPLICATION DEADLINE

SCHOLARSHIP & FINANCIAL AID INFO

DATE

COLLEGE

INITIAL IMPRESSION

POSITIVES

NEGATIVES

PROGRAMS OF STUDY

DORMS

LIBRARY

CAMPUS DINING

STUDENT LIFE

ADDITIONAL NOTES

APPLY?

APPLICATION DEADLINE

SCHOLARSHIP & FINANCIAL AID INFO

DATE

COLLEGE

INITIAL IMPRESSION

POSITIVES

NEGATIVES

PROGRAMS OF STUDY

DORMS

LIBRARY

CAMPUS DINING

STUDENT LIFE

ADDITIONAL NOTES

APPLY?

APPLICATION DEADLINE

SCHOLARSHIP & FINANCIAL AID INFO

DATE

COLLEGE

INITIAL IMPRESSION

POSITIVES

NEGATIVES

PROGRAMS OF STUDY

DORMS

LIBRARY

CAMPUS DINING

STUDENT LIFE

ADDITIONAL NOTES

APPLY?

APPLICATION DEADLINE

SCHOLARSHIP & FINANCIAL AID INFO

DATE

COLLEGE

INITIAL IMPRESSION

POSITIVES

NEGATIVES

PROGRAMS OF STUDY

DORMS

LIBRARY

CAMPUS DINING

STUDENT LIFE

ADDITIONAL NOTES

APPLY?

APPLICATION DEADLINE

SCHOLARSHIP & FINANCIAL AID INFO

DATE

COLLEGE

INITIAL IMPRESSION

POSITIVES

NEGATIVES

PROGRAMS OF STUDY

DORMS

LIBRARY

CAMPUS DINING

STUDENT LIFE

ADDITIONAL NOTES

APPLY?

APPLICATION DEADLINE

SCHOLARSHIP & FINANCIAL AID INFO

DATE

COLLEGE

INITIAL IMPRESSION

POSITIVES

NEGATIVES

PROGRAMS OF STUDY

DORMS

LIBRARY

CAMPUS DINING

STUDENT LIFE

ADDITIONAL NOTES

APPLY?

APPLICATION DEADLINE

SCHOLARSHIP & FINANCIAL AID INFO

DATE

COLLEGE

INITIAL IMPRESSION

POSITIVES

NEGATIVES

PROGRAMS OF STUDY

DORMS

LIBRARY

CAMPUS DINING

STUDENT LIFE

ADDITIONAL NOTES

APPLY?

APPLICATION DEADLINE

SCHOLARSHIP & FINANCIAL AID INFO

DATE

COLLEGE

INITIAL IMPRESSION

POSITIVES

NEGATIVES

PROGRAMS OF STUDY

DORMS

LIBRARY

CAMPUS DINING

STUDENT LIFE

ADDITIONAL NOTES

APPLY?

APPLICATION DEADLINE

SCHOLARSHIP & FINANCIAL AID INFO

DATE

COLLEGE

INITIAL IMPRESSION

POSITIVES

NEGATIVES

PROGRAMS OF STUDY

DORMS

LIBRARY

CAMPUS DINING

STUDENT LIFE

ADDITIONAL NOTES

APPLY?

APPLICATION DEADLINE

SCHOLARSHIP & FINANCIAL AID INFO

DATE

COLLEGE

INITIAL IMPRESSION

POSITIVES

NEGATIVES

PROGRAMS OF STUDY

DORMS

LIBRARY

CAMPUS DINING

STUDENT LIFE

ADDITIONAL NOTES

APPLY?

APPLICATION DEADLINE

SCHOLARSHIP & FINANCIAL AID INFO

DATE

COLLEGE

INITIAL IMPRESSION

POSITIVES

NEGATIVES

PROGRAMS OF STUDY

DORMS

LIBRARY

CAMPUS DINING

STUDENT LIFE

ADDITIONAL NOTES

APPLY?

APPLICATION DEADLINE

SCHOLARSHIP & FINANCIAL AID INFO

DATE

COLLEGE

INITIAL IMPRESSION

POSITIVES

NEGATIVES

PROGRAMS OF STUDY

DORMS

LIBRARY

CAMPUS DINING

STUDENT LIFE

ADDITIONAL NOTES

APPLY?

APPLICATION DEADLINE

SCHOLARSHIP & FINANCIAL AID INFO

DATE

COLLEGE

INITIAL IMPRESSION

POSITIVES

NEGATIVES

PROGRAMS OF STUDY

DORMS

LIBRARY

CAMPUS DINING

STUDENT LIFE

ADDITIONAL NOTES

APPLY?

APPLICATION DEADLINE

SCHOLARSHIP & FINANCIAL AID INFO

Made in the USA
Coppell, TX
24 June 2022

79214007R00056